Water on Earth

by Barbara M. Linde

Table of Contents

Introduction	2
Chapter 1 What Are the Forms of Water?	4
Chapter 2 What Is the Water Cycle?	10
Chapter 3 How Do We Get the Water We Need?	14
Chapter 4 What Is Polluted Water?	22
Summary	28
Glossary	30
Index	32

Introduction

Water is all around us. Water is in oceans, lakes, and rivers. Ice is water. Water is in the air.

▲ Earth

We need water to drink. We need water to cook and clean. We need water to live. Read this book to learn about water.

Words to Know

 condensation

 Earth

 evaporation

 gas

 liquid

 polluted

 precipitation

 solid

 water

 water vapor

See the Glossary on page 30.

Chapter 1

What Are the Forms of Water?

Water can be in three forms.
- Water can be a **liquid**.
- Water can be a **solid**.
- Water can be a **gas**.

liquid

▲ Water is in three forms.

Chapter 1

Water can be a liquid. Most liquid water on **Earth** is salt water. Salt water is in the oceans and seas.

▲ Ocean water is salt water.

Did You Know?

About ¾ of Earth's surface is water. Most water is in oceans and seas.

What Are the Forms of Water?

Fresh water is liquid water. Fresh water is water without salt.

Some fresh water is in lakes and rivers. Some fresh water is in the ground. Fresh water in the ground is ground water.

Did You Know?
Lake Baikal is the deepest lake in the world.

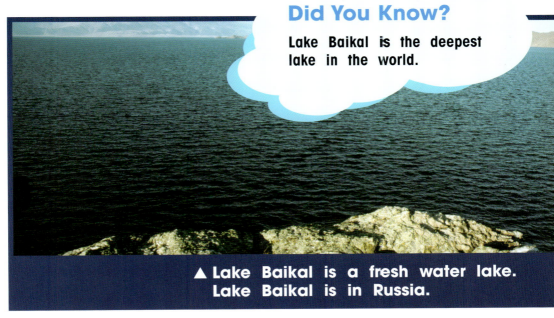
▲ Lake Baikal is a fresh water lake. Lake Baikal is in Russia.

▲ The Nile River is fresh water.

Chapter 1

Water can be a solid. Ice is solid water. Most ice is in glaciers. Glaciers are large areas of ice and snow.

Did You Know?
Most of Earth's fresh water is ice.

▲ Solid water is in glaciers.

What Are the Forms of Water?

Water can be a gas. **Water vapor** is gas. Water vapor is in the air.

▲ You can feel water vapor on your skin. Water vapor feels wet.

Chapter 2

What Is the Water Cycle?

The water cycle is the movement of water.

THE WATER CYCLE

1. The sun warms liquid water. **Evaporation** happens.

2. Water vapor rises. **Condensation** happens.

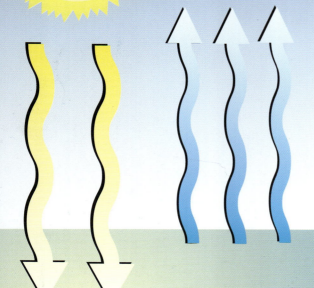

3. Tiny drops of liquid form clouds.

4. **Precipitation** falls from clouds. The precipitation falls to Earth.

Figure It Out

Look at the water cycle. What happens after step 4?

Chapter 2

Precipitation can be in many forms.

- Rain develops in warm, hot, or cool weather.

- Sleet develops in cold weather.

- Snow develops in cold weather.

- Hail usually develops in thunderstorms.

Did You Know?
Sleet is frozen rain. Hail is pieces of ice and snow.

Try This
Make a Water Cycle!

Make your own water cycle and watch it work.
- Put everything in the jar.
- Put the lid on the jar.
- Put the jar in a sunny place.
- Watch the water cycle.
- Draw pictures to show what you see.

lid
plant
water
soil
sand
pebbles

Chapter 3

How Do We Get the Water We Need?

We need fresh water to live. We need water to drink. We need water to cook and clean. We need water to grow plants.

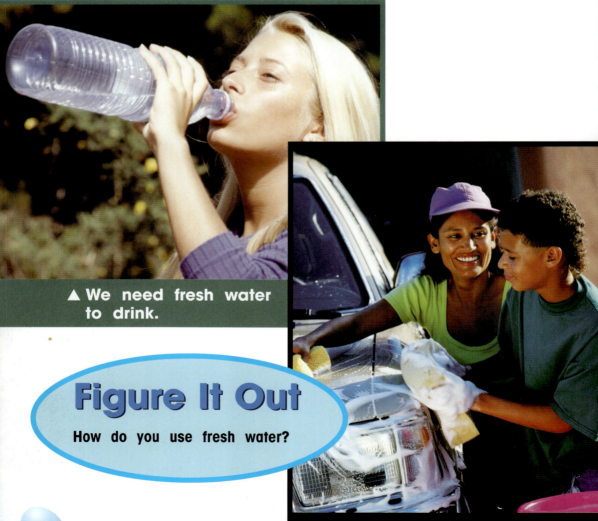

▲ We need fresh water to drink.

Figure It Out

How do you use fresh water?

▲ We use fresh water to clean.

Many people get water in their communities. People get water from a water supply system. A water supply system has three parts.

1. A water supply system has a reservoir.

▲ A reservoir is part of a water supply system.

2. A water supply system has a treatment plant.

▲ A treatment plant is part of a water supply system.

3. A water supply system has pipes.

▲ Pipes are part of a water supply system.

Chapter 3

A reservoir is part of a water supply system.

Water is pumped out of a river or lake. The water is put in a reservoir. Precipitation puts more water in the reservoir.

▲ A reservoir is a lake made by people.

How Do We Get the Water We Need?

A treatment plant is part of a water supply system.

People want to use the water in reservoirs. The water may have dirt and germs. The treatment plant cleans the water.

▲ **The treatment plant cleans reservoir water.**

Chapter 3

The water goes through a screen. Big things cannot get through the screen. Workers put good chemicals in the water. The chemicals clean the water.

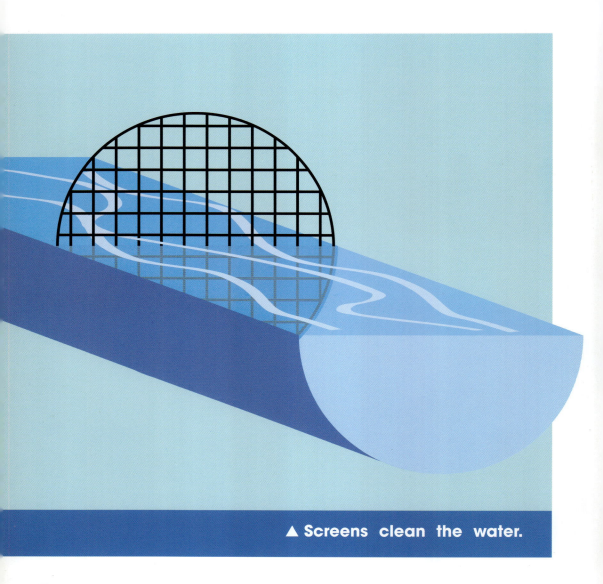

▲ Screens clean the water.

How Do We Get the Water We Need?

Pipes are part of a water supply system.

The pipes are under the ground. Water goes from the treatment plant into the pipes. The pipes take water to homes. The pipes take water to businesses and schools.

▲ Water goes through pipes into buildings.

Chapter 3

Some people are not near a water supply system. These people use ground water. Ground water is water that is in the ground.

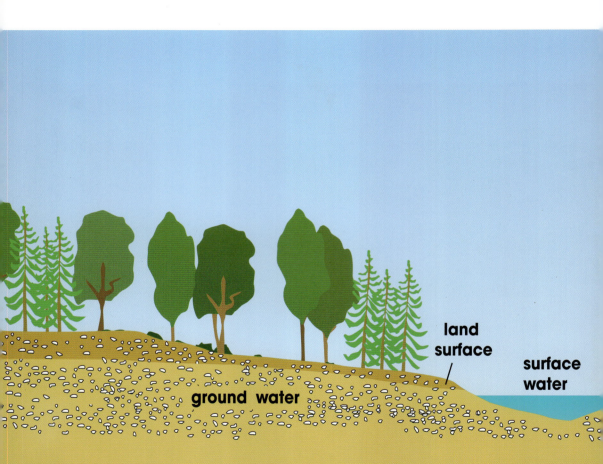

▲ Some people use water that is in the ground.

How Do We Get the Water We Need?

The people dig deep holes in the ground. The people dig holes to the ground water.

The holes are wells. People pump the water out of the wells. Often the water is clean.

▲ Water comes from wells.

Chapter 4

What Is Polluted Water?

Sometimes bad chemicals get in the water. Sometimes trash gets in the water. Then the water is **polluted** water. Polluted water is not safe to drink. Polluted water is not safe for swimming.

▲ Polluted water is not safe.

Water gets polluted in many ways. Sometimes factories spill chemicals in the water. The chemicals are poisons. Sometimes people throw trash in the water. Sometimes ships spill oil and gas in the water.

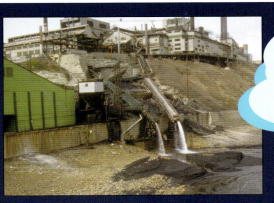

▲ Some chemicals get into the water from factories.

Did You Know?

The *Exxon Valdez* was an oil ship. The *Exxon Valdez* spilled about 11 million gallons of oil.

▲ Some trash gets into the water.

▲ Some oil and gas get into the water.

Chapter 4

Polluted water hurts animals. Fish in polluted water can get sick. The fish can die. Birds in polluted water can get sick. The birds can die.

▲ Fish in polluted water can die.

▲ Birds in polluted water can die.

What Is Polluted Water?

Some people live near polluted water. The people can get sick.

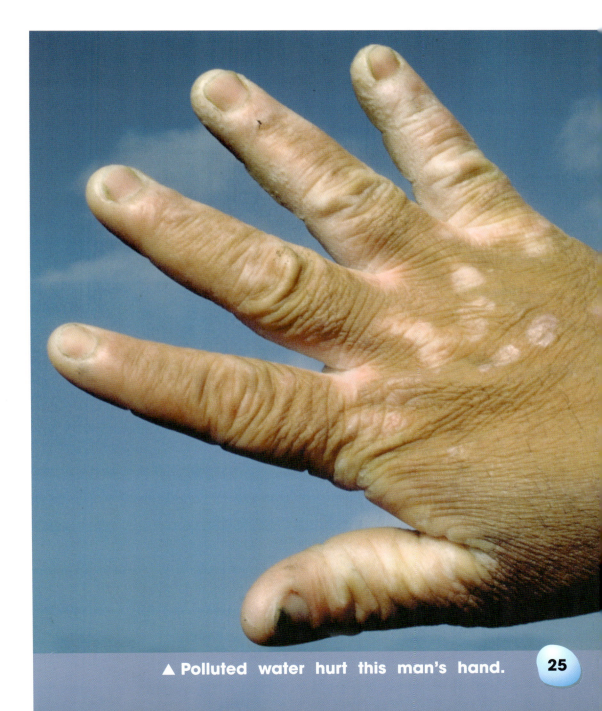

▲ Polluted water hurt this man's hand.

Chapter 4

What can you do about polluted water?
- Do not throw trash in the water.
- Pick up trash near the water.
- Do not let oil spill from a boat.
- Do not let gas spill from a boat.

What Is Polluted Water?

Solve This

Most Americans use about 50 gallons of water daily. How many gallons does each American use every month?

Answer: 1,550 gallons

It's A Fact

Earth does not get new water. Earth uses the same water again and again. The water cycle shows that Earth uses the same water.

People use Earth's water. People use much of Earth's water. How can people use less water?

1. Turn off the water when you brush your teeth.
2. Turn off the water so it does not drip.
3. Take short showers.
4. Collect rain water. Use rain water for plants.

▲ These people turned off the water.

Summary

Water is in three forms. Earth uses the same water again and again. People need clean water. Some water is polluted. Polluted water can hurt people and animals.

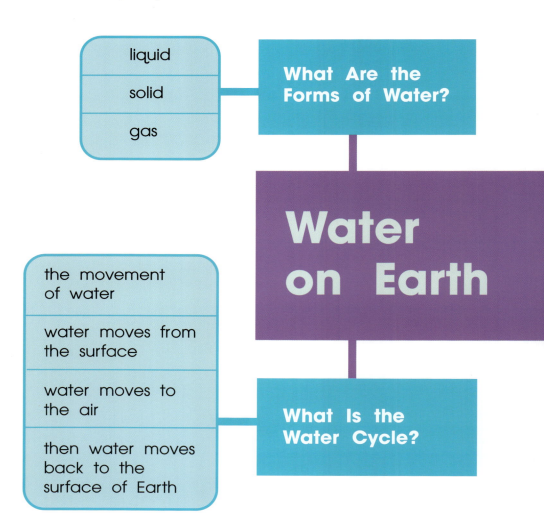

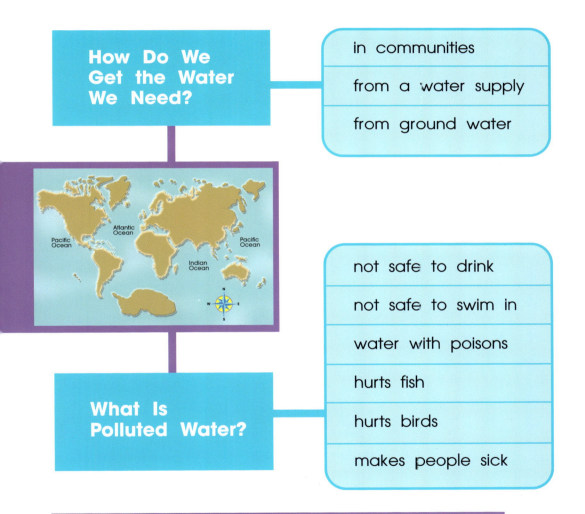

How Do We Get the Water We Need?	in communities
	from a water supply
	from ground water

What Is Polluted Water?	not safe to drink
	not safe to swim in
	water with poisons
	hurts fish
	hurts birds
	makes people sick

Think About It

1. What is the water cycle?
2. How do people get water they need?
3. How can people use less water?

Glossary

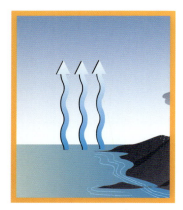

condensation when water vapor changes to a liquid

Condensation is part of the water cycle.

Earth the planet where we live

Earth has ground water.

evaporation when liquid water changes to water vapor

Evaporation is part of the water cycle.

gas a form of matter that does not have shape

Water vapor is a gas.

liquid a form of matter that does not have shape

Ocean water is a liquid.

polluted full of bad chemicals or trash

Polluted water is not safe.

precipitation water that falls from clouds to Earth

*Rain is a form of **precipitation**.*

solid a form of matter that has shape

*Ice is a **solid**.*

water a liquid, solid, or gas necessary for life on Earth

*We need **water** to live.*

water vapor water in a gas form

*You cannot see **water vapor**.*

Index

birds, 24, 29
condensation, 10
Earth, 2, 6, 8, 11, 27–28
evaporation, 10
factories, 23
fish, 24, 29
fresh water, 7–8, 14
gas, 4–5, 9, 28
glaciers, 8
ground water, 20–21, 29
hail, 12
ice, 2, 8, 12
lakes, 2, 7, 16
liquid, 4, 6, 10–11, 28
oceans, 2, 6
pipes, 15, 19
polluted, 22–26, 28–29
precipitation, 11–12, 16

rain, 12, 27
reservoir, 15–17
rivers, 2, 7, 16
salt water, 6
seas, 6
ship, 23
sleet, 12
snow, 8, 12
solid, 4–5, 8, 28
trash, 22–23, 26
treatment plant, 15, 17, 19
water, 2–4, 6–11, 13–29
water cycle, 10–11, 13, 28–29
water supply system, 15–20
water vapor, 9–10
wells, 21